The
Google
Joygle

& the accidental poetry of crowds
lawrence krauser

Warmest thanks to Terra Chalberg, Michael Collica, David Drake,
Ward Regan, Winston Rice, and Larissa Tokmakova.

ISBN 0-615-35801-2
EAN-13 978-0-615-35801-7

thejoyofg@gmail.com

Contents

THAT THIS NATION IS BECOMING

IF FISH COULD TALK THEY

BAIL OUT I SAID

THIS GINORMOUS CLOUD

AS WE ALL EMERGE

Preface

Way back in June 2008, I happened to Google the phrase **the american dream is the human dream**. Zero exact matches were returned—which at first struck me as odd. After all, it's a common idea; and during that heady, politicized spring, it danced on many tongues. But of course, there are countless ways to say the things we say.

Two months later, in late August, I searched the phrase again. This time there were two matches:

> **The American Dream is the human dream** of peace, prosperity, and the pursuit of happiness.

> **The American Dream is the human dream** intended for all, lets work together to allow other people to dream.

While it might be interesting to learn precisely when and why those seven words, in that order, entered cyberspace just when they did, I became curious about something else: the quiet but palpable sense of connection I felt when those two hits were returned.

We send a few words out into the world, and they return to us in the company of others. Usually we know what we are looking for, and have eyes for little else. I began to search a lot more, but differently, which led to this book.

*

It can be moving, how few words we need to generate resonant meaning, how quickly the general becomes personal—and how universal the personal can be. At the time of writing, the following search phrases returned the indicated number of exact matches:

if	4,410,000,000
if only	59,300,000
if only we	3,280,000
if only we would	524,000
if only we would think	19[*]
if only we would think carefully	1
if only we would think carefully about	0

That's four billion to zero—from shapeless mass to meaningful ideal—in six words flat! Of the above phrases, **if only we would think** is most pertinent to this collection. At nineteen matches, things snap into a friendly dimension. It's like reaching into a teeming sea of language, scooping up a handful and seeing what's there. Always there are surprises. We have ideas of our own about each search phrase, our own ways of completing the thought it begins; other people have other ways, contradicting as well as underscoring ours. Together, the results compose a kind of poetry of crowds, in which we can see a little of the world and a little of ourselves at the same time.

*

Here are the rules I followed when searching and editing the results:

- The search phrases were entered inside quotation marks, in order to generate only exact matches.

- The order in which the results appear is the exact order in which they appeared when the matches were returned.

- In cases where the searched phrase yielded duplicate returns, the repetitions have either been reduced to one appearance, or all have been included.

---

* See page 122.

- The paired numbers beneath each title indicate how many of the hits have been used; for example, 16/16 means that out of sixteen returned matches, all sixteen appear.

The pieces have been selected for a variety of reasons. Some are simple inventories, diverse if partial. Perhaps only a few succeed as poems. All seem most alive when read out loud, evoking mantras, litanies, theater. Throughout, there is an absence of conclusiveness—the suppression of sense exactly where one most expects to find it. While this may irk some readers, I hope it will titillate others, and even deliver a form of cognitive relief. For those of us who live day to day admid strident polemical crossfire, slowing down the rate of incoming certitude can be both tonic and provocative. Freed from their original matrices, facets of meaning flash and feint, the bulk of their intent submerged; and the key phrases tease out fresh completions in the mind.

*

While assembling this collection, I became aware of other people already doing similar things. In addition to the general bounty of works of quilted chance—from the Surrealists' "exquisite corpses" to tomorrow's virtual mashups—interested readers might especially enjoy investigating the vibrant world of Flarf (search-result poetry for which the present volume is mere primer) and the beautiful WE FEEL FINE website and book.

Lawrence Krauser

the secret of life is simple

the secret of life is simple

12/12

The secret of life is simple. It is to be true to yourself
The secret of life is simple. Breathe as long as you possibly can
The secret of life is simple. Feed the hungry, shelter the homeless
The secret of life is simple, and free of charge

The secret of life is simple : it is to throw aside the husk
THe secret of life is simple..."YOUR NOT SUPPOSE TO KNOW"
The secret of Life is simple...knowing how to enjoy the passage
remember **the secret of life is simple**: buy low and sell high

The secret of life is simple: do your own thing, and let others do their own
the secret of life is simple: if you think about something, you become it
The Secret Of Life is simple.The Secret lies within ourselves
the secret of life is simple..........there's no secret

once upon a time i was not

Once upon a time, I was not. Once upon a time, I was.
once upon a time I was not the nicest of people
Once upon a time I was not so balanced, not quite ok
Once upon a time I was not a patient person
once upon a time, I was not merely a drunk but an incontinent drunk
Once upon a time I was not Pagan

Once upon a time, I was not impressed by most synagogue music
Once upon a time I was not afraid To face this thing called life
once upon a time I was not a barbecue snob, and actually enjoyed Sonny's
Once upon a time I was not reconciled to the world
Once upon a time I was not a joiner, I guess
Once upon a time I was not quite such a veteran of fancy occasions

once upon a time I was not little Pierre at all
Once upon a time I was not in 7/8
once upon a time, I was not a vegan
Once upon a time I was not sure if I could even feel what was taking place
Once upon a time, I was not allergic to milk
Once upon a time I was not a three minute mage
Once upon a time I was not the most responsible person

Once upon a time, I was not a fan of Al Vann
Once upon a time, I was not much of a fan of single or near-single roses
Once upon a time I was not a furnace of hate
once upon a time i was not so honest
Once upon a time I was not a lawyer
shocked to hear the NBA playoffs may have been fixed **once upon a time ,**
  I was not

Once upon a time, I was not the Domestic Goddess that I am now
once upon a time i was not running following while dragging
Once upon a time I was not so musically diverse
Once upon a time I was not a patient person
Once upon a time I was NOT a fan of the show
Once upon a time, I was not well. I had weight issues

once upon a time i was not afraid to face this thing called life
Having seen you two together **once upon a time, I was not** surprised
Once upon a time I was not. Once upon a time we all were not
Once upon a time I was not frightened of the dark
Indeed, **once upon a time, I was not** terribly keen on dogs either
Once upon a time, I was not a fan

when i ask myself if i am

20/20

When I ask myself if I am okay, I usually don't know
times in every magical operation when I ask myself if I am self-deluded
when I ask myself if 'I am well?' these days, I'm able to say,
I have noticed I eat less when I ask myself if I am really hungry
when I ask myself if I am dreaming

When I ask myself if I am really happy I can answer with certainty yes or no
Let's take a look at what I think of when I ask myself if I am having fun
When I ask myself if I am treating them equally I start to feel guilty
when I ask myself if I am any more or less happy
When I ask myself if I am not trusting a Latino mechanic because he is Latino

When I ask myself if I am reallllly angry at my husband
I fall when I ask myself if I am a catalyst for unity
When I ask myself if I am giving my life my best shot
when I ask myself if I am satisfied in what I have done, at this point
when i ask myself if i am where i want to be and if i am going where i want to

When I ask myself if I am enjoying every cup of coffee made, I have to say
enjoying what I am doing but when I ask myself if I am happy
There are times when I ask myself if I am doing my part by involving myself
when I ask myself if I am understanding
when I ask myself, if I am suffering

but home for me is

but home for me is now in Knoxville, where I reside
But home for me is Google
but home for me is essentially where my family is
but home for me is Carluke
but „home" for me is about ten minutes away
But home for me is also where my mom is
But home for me is also my parents' house
but home for me is temporary until i cross atlantic shores
but home for me is still the Basque Country
but home for me is near Cambridge, where I grew up
but home for me is still my grandmother's apartment
but home for me is Belle Mead NJ
but home, for me, is Liz
but home for me is Kentucky
but home for me is in Southern Pines, NC
but home for me is Belgium
but home for me is the District
but home for me is capitol hill now
But home for me is Harvard Square
But home for me is solitude
but home for me is London
but home for me is Jeddah, Saudi Arabia and Hyderabad, India
But home for me is not a place; it is who and what
but home for me is aspatria because my best friends are there
but home for me is America
but home for me is in el dorado hills
but home for me is where family is
but home for me is New Orleans

and in a small town like ours

and in a small town like ours, you may be confronted
And in a small town like ours the woman who can earn that much money is
and in a small town like ours, it's impossible to find a writer that's not
and in a small town like ours, you can see employees using hearing protectors

And in a small town like ours, when we have only one or two guys
here and there **and in a small town like ours**, that adds up to
art **and in a small town like ours**, remarkable for its quality
and in a small town like ours, it is critical that we fill every position

and, in a small town like ours, bunk beds were unheard of
And in a small town like ours, that affects us all
and in a small town like ours, people are giving me dirty looks
and in a small town like ours you will be sorely missed

and in a small town like ours, how could that be a bad thing?
and in a small town like ours, few stayed after services
And in a small town like ours, best friends didn't come along too often
and in a small town like ours its still pretty quaint and safe

was the greatest joy of my life

THIS **WAS THE GREATEST JOY OF MY LIFE** that I've had so far!
Giving birth to my baby **was the greatest joy of my life**
At the time it **was the greatest joy of my life** and the truth is
Having both of my children **was the greatest joy of my life**,"
that smile on his family members **was the greatest joy of my life**

it **was the greatest joy of my life** to hear them tearing down the wall
It **was the greatest joy of my life** making that movie because
The discovery of time release **was the greatest joy of my life**
and that **was the greatest joy of my life** up to that time. Of course after that
It **was the greatest joy of my life** and I am sad that I gave it up

being a mother at home for a long time – which **was the greatest joy of my life** –
After a year I gave my heart to Christ It **was the greatest joy of my life**
It **was the greatest joy of my life**," he said about going to jail
I got pregnant unexpectedly and it **was the greatest joy of my life**
It **was the greatest joy of my life** -- to see how the people knew their rights

It **was the greatest joy of my life**. I always kept it safe but I had no daughters
That **was the greatest joy of my life**,' she recalled. ,But we could not be reunited
To become a grandmother **was the greatest joy of my life**
Choreographing this movie **was the greatest joy of my life**
what **was the greatest joy of my life**. I flew with him over Africa

He **was the greatest joy of my life**; until my parents were able to steal him
Nurturing my sons to manhood **was the greatest joy of my life**
finally reaching the Dodgers **was the greatest joy of my life**
it **was the greatest joy of my life** the day she told me of your love
To be able to learn and to serve **was the greatest joy of my life**

is my favorite superhero because

is my favorite superhero because he never falters

is my favorite superhero because he isn't very super

is my favorite superhero because he is a Southern gentleman with an edge

is my favorite superhero because he knows that great power comes with great responsibility

is my favorite superhero because he has a power that I can respect and hopefully attain

is my favorite superhero because he relies on intellect and stealth

is my favorite superhero because he is so incredibly Human

is my favorite superhero because he has a tough look

is my favorite superhero because for the things he had been able to accomplish despite the fact

is my favorite superhero. because of the fact the he has two sides

is my favorite superhero because he uses his super power and ability to fight for people

is my favorite superhero because he is sooo cool!!

is my favorite superhero because he's got the hottest girlfriend

is my favorite superhero because... he has the coolest power

is my favorite superhero because we have the same first name!

is my favorite superhero because he has absolutely no superpowers

is my favorite superhero because he accually has no superhero powers

is my favorite superhero because of his darkside

is my favorite superhero because he is so complex

is my favorite superhero because he can do pretty much everything

IS MY FAVORITE SUPERHERO BECAUSE HE IS LEONARDO DAVINCI

is my favorite superhero, because in spite of my age, I still wish and aspire to be like him

is my favorite superhero because he's just a badass

i saw my hope

I **saw my hope** and the God within
I **saw my hope** brighten in them
you will see what I **saw. My hope** is that this site will help

I **saw my hope** made real
and threw away whatever I **saw. My hope** is that
what I **saw...My hope** going into this game was a win

I **saw my hope** waiting for me on the kitchen table
I **saw my hope** growing less and less
I **saw my hope** and. dreams for the future

I **saw my hope**. Soon after that,
I was making of what I **saw . My hope** was to. tame my subjectivity
I **saw my hope**, as with people saw a bright light

In this fear I **saw my hope**. Was this unnatural?
I **saw my hope** revive
I **saw my hope** die as well. And now, I was holding that same hope

and in my heart i am a

and in my heart. I am a young man still
on my body **and in my heart . I am** a different person today
and in my heart I am a Buddhist although we also celebrate Islamic and Catholic
And in my heart, I am a Berliner. I'm glad to
work in my local Baptist church, **and in my heart I am a** Baptist
and in my heart, I am a Mom. So why am I not recognized
and in my heart, I am a Texan. I suffered actually more.

I am a painter by training, **and in my heart I am a** sculptor
and in my heart! I am a housewife now and I think it is just wonderful
to become united **and in my heart I am a** Yugoslav — that is the best
and in my heart I am a sissy pansy and dear friends I love sissy time!
it is in my soul **and in my heart, I am a** warrior
because I love women **and in my heart I am a** woman. So
in my mind **and in my heart i am a** winner! i scored a lot!

my dream is that someday

My dream is that someday, we will never use child abuse again
My dream is that someday we will have a more peaceful world
My dream is that someday we won't need to have a camp at all
my dream is that someday we'll work on a movie together
My dream is that someday we will be able to expand

My dream is that someday we will learn more about Cornwall
My dream is that someday we do a configurable controller
My dream is that someday we won't need IDEA
My dream is that someday we will have the statistics to show that
My dream is that someday we will be a place where we live our faith

My dream is that someday we will not see Asian, African, Indian, Caucasian
My dream is that someday we will all respect nature
My dream is that someday we don't have to be compared with men
My dream is that someday we will learn to appreciate people
My dream is that someday we'll take all these old churches and cathedrals

My dream is that someday we may be able to fight an honorable opponent
My dream is that someday we'll be able to break out of this dark strife
My dream is that someday we can create a little new contemporary committee
My dream is that someday we'll tear down a Wal-Mart to make room for
My dream is that someday we can all embrace our hair as good

My dream is that someday we can reproduce the chairs that the Tsars used
My dream is that someday we can all identify an approach
my dream is that someday we pass an Energy Bill that gives subsidies to
MY dream is that someday we can all smile upon eachother, wish eachother
my dream is that someday we can all grow beyond those silly things

13

but after i die i

20/20

but after I die I come back as a skulk
but after I die I'm forgotten, right?

But after I die, I am afraid of what would happen to him
but after I die I will be content, whether I am in heaven or hell

but after I die I will be with Jesus and that is all that matters
but after i die i dont want to cease to exist

But after I die, I,d want to talk to my Grandmother, Grandfather and Winston Churchill
But...after I die...I would want people to remember my love

but after I die..I do wonder what will happen to me
but after I die, I will definitely retire. I may even have to stop voting in N.J.

But after I die, I hope my son,s circumstances will improve
But after I die, I forget to summon him... so many wipes, man

But after I die, I will seek him out
But after I die, I don,t want the thought of me to fill my friends with pain

but after i die i just sit there a laugh about it for a sec
But after i die, i lose the weapon, which mean i have to repeat the kill

but after I die). I just don,t want some humatologist digging up my bones
But after I die I hope the people who knew me will stop to truly listen

but after i die, i want ppl to know how i felt and what my life was like
but after I die, I,m sure they,ll call me

i am honored to have been able to serve

in partnership with everyone
as Miss Black USA 2007
an institution that has made such a difference to the health of Texas
as INFORMS Vice President of Information
in that capacity
my country and to help
as its Chancellor for four years
our local community for so long
the people of District 2 since 1996
as the Co-Chair for this event
Montana as Attorney General
our residents for the past four years
as an AdvisorMax Expert
it
as the supervisor of officials all these years
with him and even more honored to have been able to call him my friend
in a small way
the membership of CCML in this capacity
the Council in this role
as chair of the Applied Probability Society
with. those 3rd and 4th generation family members
as provost, but it is time to get back

the best thing I ever did by far

sex for me has always been

20/20

sex for me has always been with someone I'm in love with
The best **sex for me has always been** in the context of a monogamous
Sex for me has always been a terribly important part of life
Sex for me has always been an expression of lust and love
Sex for me has always been better when there is a touch of affection involved

when I say that **sex for me has always been** about
Sex for me has always been, and will always be, an expression of love
Sex for me has always been the other person's pleasure
I have to say that **sex for me has always been** more of an intimacy thing
so **sex for me has always been** something beautiful, fun, exciting

Sex for me has always been psychological
Sex for me has always been too intense to remain casual about
Sex for me has always been a positive and pleasant enterprise
Sex, for me, has always been considered the act of orgasm
Sex for me has always been so "hush, hush" and "behind close doors

Sex for me has always been a huge part of my extracurricular activities
Sex, for me, has always been an active, energetic connection with the Cosmic
Sex for me has always been about making my partner happy
Sex for me, has always been important
sex for me has always been totally blatant

the best thing i ever did by far

It's **the best thing I ever did, by far**. It's also the hardest
it's **the best thing I ever did by far**, I love my teeth
Besides marrying my husband and having my two beautiful sons this is **the best
thing I ever did (BY FAR)**
the best thing I ever did by far was to to give my life to the Lord
Becoming a mom was absolutely **the best thing I ever did. By far**

were talking, the sun

12/12

We **were talking, the sun** had already gone down
While we **were talking, the sun** went down and the stars came out
As we **were talking the sun** went behind the mountains

While they **were talking, the sun** rose and shone pleasantly into the prison
While the three **were talking, the sun** has sunk lower and lower

Now while we **were talking the sun** had sunk swiftly
We **were talking, the sun** had already gone down, but the sky had yet to light up
While we **were talking the sun** came out for about 20 minutes

trees themselves **were talking. The sun** was showing a little gig

While we **were talking the sun** came out from behind the thick cloud cover and
As we **were talking the sun** came out and it became a glorious day

While we **were talking, the sun** set

fingers on that guitar

17/17

worked out the **fingers on that guitar** tonight

the minute he put his **fingers on that guitar**, that was it
can meld any song to his magical **fingers on that guitar**

He had magical **fingers on that guitar**
I wore off five sets of **fingers on that guitar**
the way you work your magical **fingers on that guitar** of yours is just outstanding

The guy must have magical **fingers on that guitar**!
those **fingers on that guitar** and the piano!! yumm!!
a backbeat part where I'm just plucking with my **fingers on that guitar**
creates a current through his soul into his **fingers on that guitar**
i'd have sex with his **fingers on that guitar**!!!

She expresses all her feelings through her **fingers on that guitar**
So I cleared my throat and placed my **fingers on that guitar**
some flying **fingers on that guitar**!

and the way she used her **fingers on that guitar** is awesome
Man, I love the **fingers on that guitar**

His **fingers on that guitar**… Ohhhhh… I'm SO jealous of that guitar!!!!!

feeling inside growing

the restlessness he was **feeling inside growing** with each
feeling inside, growing ever stronger. I can't deny it. Soon
I get a warm, glowing **feeling inside. Growing** up in the early 80s,

Hiding the **feeling inside ... growing** so strong, I can't wait
here's a new **feeling inside growing**. And this smile just
getting this **feeling inside growing** up again that I should

if this is true, this **feeling inside growing** within me is pure and
hysterical b-b-be **feeling inside growing** of me was like i bigger was
oh, This bubbly **feeling inside, Growing**, growing, This feeling

The **feeling inside growing** and shinning. I can't help but smile
watched her sleep, the **feeling inside growing** at each turn of
sahaja yoga Have you ever felt a **feeling inside? Growing** deep

into my ears, I left immediately, with the **feeling inside growing**
and the sloshy **feeling inside growing** more intense with the commute
This **feeling inside growing**, spreading, takeing hold until my

forien **feeling inside growing**, just like a plague. I'm tired of
smiling and with that weird **feeling inside. Growing** up i listen
on fire too, that **feeling inside growing** so big I almost do

remember every hour of

30/30

I **remember every hour of** our ritual, and there is a ritual for every hour
I **remember every hour of** every single day
Do you **remember every hour of** your life?

Remember, every hour of thy time is a part of thy treasure
There are a thousand details to **remember every hour of** every day
(**remember every hour of** driving time is an hour less of good operating time)

I think I can **remember every hour of** that year
God desires that we **remember every hour of** our lives
getting elected will require you to **remember, every hour of** every day

Remember, every hour of sleep prior to midnight is worth two hours after
Help me **remember every hour of** every day
Do you **remember every hour of** your life?" „No I don't."

remember every hour of the day that he has but one duty
I do **remember every hour Of** that sweet comradeship!
Fourteen years and yet I **remember every hour of** that day

sounds I will always **remember. Every hour of** every day
He could **remember every hour of** his life
You will **remember every hour of** the past

True, we cannot **remember every hour of** the day
remember, every hour of lecture you miss is really 3 hours of alone study
I think I **remember every hour of** every day I spent at camp

Remember, every hour of work is an hour closer to beer
I think I will **remember every hour of** that day
I can **remember every hour of** the 21 days I spent in Bhutan

remember, every hour of work lost is another hour of you must spend to replace
something which I still **remember, every hour of** my time is worth $2
but I can **remember every hour of** Wingspread

perfecting essays and trying to **remember every hour of** volunteering
to **remember every hour of** the day: You must not speak
Yes, I **remember every hour of** that day

spoke this single word

8/8

three stones cradled in the exhausted spring **spoke this single word**
His voice was soft as a feather as he **spoke this single word**
she **spoke this single word** raw, without a break
Sounding very confused as he **spoke this single word**
stood beside him **spoke this single word**; his name
hate and scorn in her voice as she **spoke this single word**
who but **spoke this single word**: Necam, which means revenge
Even as she **spoke this single word**, her voice rose in pitch

at the lobe of my ear

nibbles **at the lobe of my ear** so I'm slightly excited
at the lobe of my ear due to the unavoidable damage to the facial nerve
nipped **at the lobe of my ear** and chuckled
slight tug **at the lobe of my ear** telling me that, no, i am
wet and rough run slowly up my neck to tug **at the lobe of my ear**
nip sharply **at the lobe of my ear**, "I lied" A thrill
start to nibble **at the lobe of my ear** as the blood starts to run

and when we made love we

together **and when we made love we** made love
type **and when we made love we** often inflamed each other
honey, **and when we made love we** both came until we
head **and when we made love we** use to talk about it and
do, **and when we made love, we** did it without abandon

time was moving like

5/5

Time was moving like cane molasses
if these images were in real **time, was moving like**
time was moving like an old snail
and the **time was moving like** before but of course not
and **time was moving like** a farting tortoise

tickly torture

luckily, after a bit of **tickly torture**, this time it worked:
Her feet are basically, totally helpless to the **tickly torture**

in this epic tale of top heavy **tickly torture**
whether the **tickly torture** is just a less intense version of pain
he was released and the **tickly torture** on his skin was making
the drummy Elfman music. It's almost crosses into **tickly torture**

Feathers are a really annoying **tickly torture** I find
tickly torture the cuddly arm all the stories, like the
time my baby latches on, it's a skin crawling **tickly torture**
(they'll play **tickly torture** or tickly tackle, but no hitting)

Oh noes! Aren't the worms enough t**tickly torture**?
An infinite loop of pure **tickly torture**! X3 I luv it!

after her **tickly torture**, unaware of what her heaving chest was doing
I managed to control myself despite it being **tickly torture**
at least until they made me laugh with **tickly torture**, I
do believe I still have those **tickly torture** feathers about...

Tickly torture or something
some sort of foxy **tickly torture**...or just saying
Go Rio! Give him a **tickly torture** to remember!

having to **tickly torture**
FEEL THE **tickly torture**!
He had to brave a light **tickly torture**

My **Tickly Torture** part 2 (m/m)
spy tied tickle - ENTER HERE **tickly torture**
tickly torture fetish stories movies fucked hogtied free
and glad to be back to a place of comfort, giggles and **tickly torture**

tickly foot | tickly girl | tickly soles | tickly toes | **tickly torture**
unbearably ticklish toes | fetish tickling | **tickly torture**

tickly torture - In position and had to withstand

erotic tickling movies | tickling tootsies | **tickly torture**
celebrities tickling | tickle her feet with feather | **tickly torture**
tickling orgasms videos | tickling her stomach | **tickly torture**
friend story | **tickly torture** | tickling armpits mercy ticklish forever

the promised land in sight

matrix degradation: is **the promised land in sight**?

waves of immigrants to **the promised land. In sight** of the Statute of Liberty,
fired with an evangelical zeal, they could see **the promised land in sight**
Then, **the Promised Land in sight**, at long last, at long last, they begin

The promised land in sight when Murtagh pointed two late frees to leave
Summit Plateau with **the promised land in sight**. Again, enlarge this picture
Off the Chinese coast he died, with **the promised land in sight**
with **the promised land in sight**, nobody wanted to risk missing out

now at the river's edge, with **the Promised Land in sight**
standing on the banks of the Jordon with **the promised land in sight**
they need to work for the full 90 minutes to keep **the promised land in sight**

They had **the promised land in sight** when fear took over. They said,
To **the promised land in sight**. Verse 3
in Deuteronomy: . 1:19-22. **The promised land in sight**

after the hard desert journey and **the Promised Land in sight**
Israel and God make out **The Promised Land in sight**. The passage
now is **the promised land in sight**. Skyland!

He was held a prisoner for three days, with **the promised land in sight**
an older man who had come to retire in **the promised land in sight** of the temple
With **the Promised Land in sight**, the Democrats nominated Grover Cleveland
the promising athlete who gets derailed with **the promised land in sight**

Is **the promised land in sight**? The folks at Free the Hops say
We had **the promised land in sight** and yet were disappointed
before **the promised land in sight** of which the prophet of God must die
Moses dies, **the Promised Land in sight**. Paul reaches. Rome

With **the Promised Land in sight**, there was need for all resources to be
swept into **the Promised Land. In sight** of Jebel Mussa
Moses has just died in the wilderness, with **the Promised Land in sight**

Off Roanoke, **the promised land in sight**, Hailing its shores with rapturous
wandering in the desert Nebo **the promised land in sight**

Dammit, Mike, I have **the Promised Land in sight**
How loomed **the promised land in sight** !

i love you because you always

86/86

I love you because you always makes me smile • I love you because you always tell me how lucky you are to be with me • I love you because you always try to make birthdays a special event • I love you because you always without fail fall over • I love you because you always made me breakfast in high school • I love you because you always say, "I love you," • i love you because you always support me in everything i do • I love you because you always speak your mind • i love you because you always have my back lord • I Love You Because...You always don't agree with me • I love you because you always put Elizabeth and I first • I love you because you always give me the benefit of the doubt • I love you because you always make me feel happy whenever I talk to you • I love you because you always remained true to yourself and to me • I love you because you always know what to say to make me laugh • I love you because you always comfort me or give me a shoulder to cry on • I love you because you always listen • I love you because you always seem to cope • I love you because you always leave a big tip • i love you because you always have food :) • I LOVE YOU BECAUSE YOU ALWAYS KNOW THE RIGHT WORDS TO " SAY " • I love you because you always chill outside wid me • I love you because you always seemed to water and feed my • "I love you BECAUSE you always put out • I love you because you always hold me close to you • I love you because you always have the last word • I love you because you always know how to make me laugh • I love you because you always see the good in people • I love you because you always fall when you run • I love you because you always. smile when our eyes meet • I love you because you always help me with my homework • i love you because you always take tha time • I love you because you always remember to bring the fish oil • I love you because you always hold me when I'm sad • I love you because you always look like a hawt manaquin • I LOVE YOU . Because you always know what to say • "I Love You", because you always do things for them that after a while • I love you because you always supply the best Kate stuff • omg i love you, because you always have the website • I love you because you always did the best you could • I love you because you always bother my nights • "I love you"because you always support me • i love you

34

because you always make awesome photos ! • **I love you because you always** listen to my innocent and silly feelings • **I love you because you always** tell me how lucky you are to be with me • **I love you because you always** take care of people around you • **I LOVE YOU - because you always** say what I need to hear • **I Love You Because; You Always** Hurt The One You Love • I love you, not **I love you because you always** • **I love you because you always** manage to cheer me up • **I love you because you always** say the right things • its hard to say **i love you because you always** say " you don't mean it. • **i love you because you always** make me laugh • **i love you because you always** provide us such GREAT, pics • **I love you because you always** listen to your fans • **I love you because you always** makeme laugh and your so nice • **I love you because you always** know just what I need • **I love you because you always** find the candy store • **I Love You-- because you always** bring up something that is so "TRUE • **I love you because you always** believe in me • **I love you because you always** have a smile on your face • **i love you because you always** smile • **I love you because you always** make me smile and even if • **I love you, because you always** remembered our anniversary • i should tell you **i love you because you always** tell me • **i love you because you always** take my side • **I love you because you always** know what to say • **I love you because you always** make me happy • **I love you because you always** knock common sense into me • **I love you, because you always** protect me • **I love you because you always** motivate me to study hard! • **I Love You because you always** color in my mind • **I love you because you always** think of the really best, wonderful things • **I love you, because You always** love me • **I love you because you always** seem to be happy • **I love you. Because you always**, always, always write • **i love you because you always** sound like • **I love you because you always** put a smile on my face • **I love you because you always** sound excited to hear from me & & & • **i love you, because you always** make those scratchy noises • **I love you because you always** say • **I love you because you always** think • **I love you because you always** shower • **I LOVE YOU because you always** wanted your family to be happy • **I love you.. because you always** hear my silly stories • **i love you because you always** make me wanna

that this nation is becoming

the situation over there now

u stil with d lads or wats **the situation over there now**?

The situation over there now is so very desperate for both sides
nor does it do a good job of explaining **the situation over there now**
that **the situation over there now** is pretty grim and dangerous

How is **the situation over there now** ?
how is **the situation over there now** with Rascism?
will this be accomplished without further inflaming **the situation over there now**?
do you think they are in control of **the situation over there now**?
What is **the situation over there now**? What's it like?
What do you think of **the situation over there now**?

i think **the situation over there now** is ridiculous and a horrible disaster

So hows **the situation over there now**? Any Impt updates?

please stop downplaying **the situation over there now**

How is **the situation over there now**? Do you recommend to go there for surfing

I certainly don't think we can just turn our backs on **the situation over there now**
I'm really getting worried, because of **the situation over there now**

bitter enemies standing

8/8

Imagine your **bitter enemies standing** in awe of you
bitter enemies standing at opposite ends of the green
There they were, all the **bitter enemies standing** together
Sunrise the next morning saw once **bitter enemies standing** side-by-side
people who, in his mind, are **bitter enemies, standing** in such close proximity
forged in battle, **bitter enemies standing** back-to-back
former friends, now **bitter enemies. Standing** toe to toe
was two **bitter enemies standing** united

every year the storms

11/11

when **every year the storms** return
Every year, the storms, the cold and the poor
every year the storms get bigger and so do the insurance claims
but **every year the storms** rose up again

every year the storms could be miles away , I run
20 typhoons and storms **every year. The storms** bring floods

every year the storms are getting stronger and stronger
Every year the storms come through and change the landscape
Every year the storms got smaller

It started getting warmer **every year. The storms** got worse
Every year the storms, which are becoming increasingly frequent

exploding every hour

14/14

three ten-megaton bombs **exploding every hour**
fantastic volcano welcomes guests by **exploding every hour**
This movement is **exploding every hour**, lets keep this Revolution Alive
with tires **exploding every hour** and engines going wrong every three

the equivalent of three 10 megaton bombs **exploding every hour**
an "oversight hearing" **exploding every hour**
couldn't sleep, especially with all the bombs **exploding every hour**

if that were true, there's be millions of people **exploding every hour**
exploding every hour. Little did residents of New York and New England know
a strong hurricane is comparable to a 30 Megaton nuclear bomb **exploding every
hour**

as long as her little bum isnt **exploding every hour**
which is **exploding every hour** with tons and tons of faves
Famous for **exploding EVERY hour**, ON the hour!"
exploding every hour in reminder of the pleasure denied me

was a snake pit of

Christian Europe **was a snake pit of** bigotry up until the 16th Century
her halfway house **was a snake pit of** drugs, alcohol, sex and terror
her court **was a snake-pit of** favourites and sycophants

Though warned that DOE **was "a snake pit" of** problems
his court **was a snake pit of**seething ambitions and relentless plotting
The office **was a snake pit of** jealousy and indulgence
Underneath the desk **was a snake pit of** tangled cords

History, it seemed, **was a snake pit of** turning points
was a snake pit of warring factions, revolutionary governments,
    and corrupt system governors
this place **was a snake pit of** warring egos
was a snake pit of running children, ear-shattering "music

Nazi Germany **was a snake pit of** political infighting
was a snake pit ofintrigue and tragic comedy

the Roosevelt administration **was a snake pit of** influential leaders
    and faceless bureaucrats

My shoulder **was a snake pit of** laxity and tears
was a snake pit of internecine strife between poets. and fiction writers
was a snake pit of marital infidelities, sex with inmates and staff
was a snake pit of bigotry up until the 16th Century

that this nation is becoming

Could it be **that this nation is becoming** colorblind
seeing **that this nation is becoming** more and more fascist,
to deny **that this nation is becoming** a financial oligarchy
Could it be **that this nation is becoming** colorblind

the reality **that this nation is becoming** a land of those who have a lot
this just add to the police state **that this nation is becoming**

I don't need to tell anyone **that this nation is becoming** more diverse

a sad sad state of affairs **that this nation is becoming** one nation under debt

I believe **that this nation is becoming** too computer dependent
that this nation is becoming everything we have fought wars over NOT to become

I agree **that this nation is becoming** wussified
that this nation is becoming more and more dependent on minerals
the heads of these would-be superiors the fact **that this nation is becoming**
that this nation is becoming dominated by the investor class

that this nation is becoming a growing mission field day by day
he must conclude **that this nation is becoming** "post-civilized
Could it be **that this nation is becoming** colorblind

data **that this nation is becoming** known by
terrible family violence data **that this nation is becoming** known for

I am increasingly troubled **that this nation is becoming** increasingly preoccupied

it will be the brown-shirts **that this nation is becoming**

that this nation is becoming obsessed with trying to make a quick buck
this scenario suggests **that this nation is becoming** increasingly dependent
that this nation is becoming increasingly politically unstable
that this nation is becoming the Old Europe against which our new nation
that this nation is becoming actually a republic in which the workingmen
I submit **that this nation is becoming** wimps in terms of dealing

what health care what

What banks **what health care**? **What** are you talking about?
Who shall receive **what health care**? **What** resources
what health care, **what** coverage, charging
WHAT health care? **What** is there to stay for?
what jobs, what home, **what health care**, **what** hope
What health care? **What** social security?
reform **what**? **Health care**? **What**?

was a president we

was a President. We had
was a President we could be proud of
was a president we could take pride in when he traveled

I could feel that he **was a president we** can do business with
was a president "we had heard woke up every morning and asked to do God's will
now there **was a president we** liked

was a President we would NOT call great, and never call honest
was a President we expect better from
he **was a president we** never saw in his wheelchair

If there **was a president . . . we** would walk even tonight
That **was a president we** heard tonight
was a President we all can be proud of and one who is proud

slogan **was, "A President we** won't have to train." Sound familiar?
didn't know there **was a president. We** were told the outside world was evil
when he **was a president, we** would have done the same

And because he **was a president we** can also say that it was politically motivated
if it **was a President we** actually liked we'd have been even more excited
If it **was a President we** liked (or, at least could tolerate) I'd want them to be just

pro life bitch/pro choice bitch

23/23 & 23/23, interwoven

Pro-life Bitch
Pro CHOICE bitch!
Crazy **Pro-life Bitch**. Hello
wow what a crazy **pro-choice bitch**
Crazy **pro-life bitch** seizuring during a protest
I am **pro-choice, bitch** at me all you want
She is a nut job **pro life bitch** who
ging to smash **pro choice bitch´s** soon!
fanatic **pro life bitch**
AHAHAHA **PRO CHOICE BITCH** !!!
Re: fanatic **pro life bitch**
mother, internet blogger, opinionated, feminist, **pro choice, bitch**
Deignan is **pro-life; Bitch** Ph.D. is pro-choice
I am **pro-choice, bitch**
gestapo should arrest this vile little **pro-life bitch**
playing baby daughter to a **pro- choice bitch**!
Creationist, environmental despoiler,and **pro-life bitch** of a
I'm **pro-choice bitch**, are you pro-life? OOps!
lucky she won in Alaska the Pro life bitch
because you like fucking republicans **pro choice bitch**
f-ing **pro-life bitch**
YOU EVIL ANTI **PRO CHOICE BITCH** [info]
A **pro-life bitch** just might be our first female
damn if she ain't **pro choice, bitch** never used a condom
life liberty pursuit of happiness **pro life bitch**
would be simple for some bloody-wombed **pro-choice bitch**
Impregnate a **pro-life bitch** then
but only if that woman is a liberal **pro-choice bitch**
Honk for **pro life - BITCH**! Wow!
What do you mean you're **pro-choice, bitch**?

if ya ain't **pro life bitch**.......then ummm don't start
uuuugly, liberal, **pro-choice bitch** from code pink
[TRANSLATED] Crazy **Pro-life Bitch**. 14 seconds of ecstacy!
yeah, so i'm a **pro-choice bitch**
nearly ruined by the **pro-life bitch**
Get Educated! I'm **Pro-Choice Bitch**!
Fuck that **Pro Life bitch**!
You better be **pro-choice bitch**!
Crazy **Pro-life Bitch**. bitch screaming
I'm a snarky, rabidly **pro-choice bitch**
the **pro-life bitch** camped out and was bit by an angry beaver
I already said im **pro-choice bitch**!
a little secret: **PRO-LIFE, bitch**. Get it?
As many of you know, this **pro-choice bitch** volunteers
Repulsive, disgusting fanatical-Catholic **pro-life bitch**
I'm fucking **pro-choice bitch**. Do you support the death penalty?

that darned freedom

16/16

That darned "**freedom** of speech" thing always gets in the way
I think you're in cahoots with **that darned Freedom** Cat!
(there I go using **that darned freedom** of choice thing again
that darned Freedom of Religion thing gets in the way of a good jihad

That darned freedom. It makes people do such strange things.
That darned freedom of information act). Thank you to all of you for getting this info
because of **that darned freedom** of religion bit of the Constitution
It's **that darned Freedom** of Speech thing...

But **that darned freedom** of speech thing get's in the way ... again!
that darned freedom of movement thing in the USA, diluting
That darned freedom of speech thing... Now
and **that darned freedom** of speech and will continue to voice

Wow, **that darned freedom** of speech thing just seems to just
That darned freedom of speach thing just bites you in the ass
would somebody please do something about **that darned freedom**
That darned freedom of speech can sure get in the way

50

how many teabag

Re: **how many teabag** protestors has obama arrested?
How many teabag threads are there? Consolidate!!
Just wondering **how many "teabag** patriots" even know about
How many Teabag movement people do you know personally?

One possible problem is **how many teabag** sympathizers
know how much a packet costs and **how many teabag** are in 1 packet
How many teabag meetings have you been to?

Question? **How many teabag** meetings have you been to?
(now **how many teabag** jokes do you think there are going to be?)

how many teabag party attendees suckle at the public teat,
I wonder **how many Teabag** men rollover @ night,
How many teabag parties were in Texas?

How many Teabag Birthers does it take to
prove **how many teabag** protestors were supposedly on the Mall

How many #teabag parties are going on today? And
how many teabag parties were there between 2000 and
rambo, or **how many teabag** parties you've sponsored, mr. paine

?! **how many Teabag** related emergencies are there, really?!!
On the other hand, **how many Teabag** women roll over @ night

How many teabag party contributions will be made by people
How many teabag inbred relatives does it take to...no...

for sure but the good news
20/20

long film, that's **for sure. But the good news** is that the story moves
now **for sure, but the good news** is that the stuff is almost ready
I can't say that **for sure. But the good news** is he did show a lot of flash
a lot there **for sure, but the good news** is that someone's starting to realize

We got tested on Friday, that's **for sure. But the good news** is that we had
Not the best timing, **for sure, but the good news** you have a well-tuned
favorite bird **for sure. But the good news** doesn't end there
hd-dvd looks bleak **for sure. But the good news** is, my hd-a30 is

not going to be a very pleasant day out, **for sure, but the good news**
for sure but the good news is the cruises to the beach in the future wont be
Disappointed **for sure....but the good news**
Was not what I expected **for sure but the good news**?

for sure, but the good news is that there are many
Bad memories **for sure, but the good news** is that none of that happens in Portuguese
a tongue twister **for sure, but the good news** is that
you'll need the hat and gloves **for sure! But, the good news** is that

I will fall short **for sure but the good news** is I know my savior
In my dreams, that's **for sure. But the good news** is we can go online
go down as one of my top 10, that's **for sure. But the good news** is
We don't know this **for sure. But the good news** is we only have to wait

and that's just one reason why we

And that's just one reason why we're so proud to be part of the Cat Blogosphere
And that's just one reason why we're inviting you to participate
And that's just one reason why we're the preferred South Florida Florist
and that's just one reason why we heart him so

and that's just one reason why we need a diversity of grocery stores
and that's just one reason why we think that Bill Clinton is fascinating
And that's just one reason why we should encourage the royal family to
and that's just one reason why we sell more life insurance than any other

And that's just one reason why we love exploring the >Jewish roots!
And that's just one reason why we cover Tampa's social scene
and that's just one reason why we chose them for this project
Yes, **and that's just one reason why we** love them

And that's just one reason why we find him so cool
And that's just one reason why we don't have the option

If fish could talk they

please tell me everything
you know about the

the Russian Mafia

the first few days of heroin withdrawal

the game Unreal Tournament

the upcoming Gymnastics Tour!?

the yamabushi!

the missing money

the American Revolution

the fire at your warehouse

the Hinckley Scholarship

the fire

the watchers

the game

the falcon?

the Tree Streets area

the subject!

the butterfly bush

the fourth picture in the slideshow

the surname such-and-such

the title 'Princess Royal'

the Diplocaulus?

the Hidden 3 sec CD on WF procs?

the United Arab Emirates!

the preservre resort

the way the Verizon contract will work

the company

the Grinch

the character

the next Gen Prius

the change of ownership

the string and M theories

the freshwater angelfish

the solution

the family who formed

8/8

the eldest brother of **the family who formed** the group, became
a friend of **the family who formed** the support group
of **the family who formed** the group
on the rest of **the family, who formed** a coalition against her
to integrate **the family, who formed** coalitions
who failed to integrate **the family, who formed**
members of **the family who formed** the orchestra for
the eldest brother of **the family who formed** the group

people with all the time in the world

25/25

the low income or elderly not two young **people with all the time in the world**
who cares if a few "**people with all the time in the world** have a few opinions
people with all the time in the world and brilliant staffs of clerks
people with all the time in the world who are incapable of taking a fresh look
great for **people with all the time in the world** – preferably those who are reclusive

Ahhh, those young **people with all the time in the world** to recover
there are some **people with all the time in the world** who tend to report offenders
old people, retired people, **people with all the time in the world**
being driven crazy by **people with all the time in the world**
Unoccupied **people with all the time in the world** want WORK

unbearable to wait behind **people with all the time in the world**
People with all the time in the world don't have to worry
People with all the time in the world are just padding the numbers
that are going to baffle the wisest of **people with all the time in the world**
People with all the time in the world have tons of gold sitting around

Lures are for **people with all the time in the world**
people with all the time in the world on their hands are nut cases
if **people with all the time in the world** on their hands actually did something
smart **people with all the time in the world** to answer your tax questions
Here are some interesting links for **people with all the time in the world**

people with all the time in the world, seated in comfortable nonthreatening
   surroundings
And **people with all the time in the world** dont appreciate it
do not have the option to act like **people with all the time in the world**
gregarious **people with all the time in the world** to get from point A to point B
I am one of those **people with all the time in the world**

number of rats in the city

we can never really know the exact **number of rats in the city**
To minimize the **number of rats in the City**
management and collection, illegal dumping and **number of rats in the city**
the **number of rats in the city** "does seem to be on the decline

the **number of rats in the city** had dropped from two per person
Whether that has increased the **number of rats in the city** is anyone's guess
Officials could not estimate the **number of rats in the city**, but
the exact **number of rats in the city**, based on the number of fumigated rat holes

has said the increased **number of rats in the city** doesn't pose a health risk but
high with rubbish bags, which again led to a boom in the **number of rats in the city**
the lack of weekly collections has led to a rise in the **number of rats in the city**
The **number of rats in the city** has grown 20 percent in less than six years

reduce the **number of rats in the city**
deal with the **number of rats in the city**

what books will do

I have a great example of **what books will do** for someone
But no one agrees as to just **what books will do** this. The
world, thats **what books will do** for you

Fearful of **what books will do** to him, Rich
knew **what books will do** to people,
what trash is and **what books will do** well
what books will do for a man, and what a thinker will

seen the cave paintings

18/18

night had never **seen the cave's paintings**
Would have liked to have **seen the cave paintings** which were not on view
We had **seen the cave paintings** first time about 36 years back

If you have **seen the cave paintings**, they depict a new story
but I was sure she had never **seen the cave paintings**

I've **seen the cave paintings** at Lascaux and other places
Maybe there we could have **seen the cave paintings**.

Anyone who has **seen the cave paintings** in Europe, Africa, Australia, or
If you've **seen the cave paintings** shown for ancient man
no intrinsic value or purpose but might have **seen the cave paintings** as art

We've **seen the cave paintings**, but there are no recordings, of course
seen the cave paintings at Alta-. mira cannot fail to be impressed
I've **seen the cave paintings**....hunting, killing

she laughed back, "Have you ever **seen the cave paintings** in France?
climbed Sigiriya and and **seen the cave paintings**
Or **seen the cave paintings** in Lascaux

Scientists have **seen the cave paintings**, their exact words were
Now I've **seen the cave paintings** of him in the old part of the canyon

but the coolest thing about them is

But the coolest thing about them is that some of these aren't developed
but the coolest thing about them is that none of their music is messed with
but the coolest thing about them is they all tell students "You guys will be fine
but the coolest thing about them is that they come in multiple sizes

but the coolest thing about them is that they are viewer created!
but the coolest thing about them is that THEIR MUM'S THINK THEY
   ARE SO COOL
but the coolest thing about them is that I don't think they've changed
But the coolest thing about them is the white spot on each side of their heads

but the coolest thing about them is that my kids are fascinated by the amazing
plastic bag for freshness and convenience, **but the coolest thing about them is**
stylish and sexy, **but the coolest thing about them is** the reasonable price
but the coolest thing about them is that they have these changable seats that

look great as they are, **but the coolest thing about them is**
They are the most PIMP shoes available, **but the coolest thing about them is**
But the coolest thing about them is their many additional nutrients
but the coolest thing about them is animation and for that you'll need a strobe

every single country in this world

because it used by practically **ESCITW**
people can be happy in **ESCITW**, and
ESCITW depends on USA economy (OK, maybe
ESCITW has delicious cuisine and also
ESCITW declared war on America they'd beat us
and I am a coward because **ESCITW** lacks democracy!
ESCITW has a history that is full of pride and
ESCITW has designed its own specific, unique flag
ESCITW knows that they are not going to be prosecuted
according to **ESCITW** except for the loyal puppy
can get women from **ESCITW** pregnant when
ESCITW is harboring terrorists, including America.
ESCITW has pedophiles, rapists, murderers,
which phenomenon, in my opinion, exists in **ESCITW**,
what you call "repression", then I think that's what **ESCITW**
ESCITW has the right to develope nuclear technology for
relationship with Iran and for that matter with **ESCITW**,
ESCITW is controlled by his respective zodiacal symbol
and pretty much **ESCITW**. American isn't a race. That's
why your found in **ESCITW** , separated and humalated ,
ESCITW, except for Iran, is enslaved in debt to
ESCITW. It impacts you you and you. It impacts
this world if **ESCITW** used energy and emitted
that **ESCITW** is only after their own interest. Even
iPods & iPhones are greedily lapped up by **ESCITW**
hek! it s illegal in **ESCITW** except for lebanon!
doubt you've been to **ESCITW**. Anyone who has wouldn't
invade and nation build **ESCITW** where there are terrorists
If that's your logic....**ESCITW** would want to have a team
and im sure that show has woman from **ESCITW**

a very dangerous game for all of us, for **ESCITW**
recognized by almost **ESCITW** is pizza. In the past
ESCITW trades. You might know more about
ESCITW do Eminent domain. Some more than others
having more power and pretty much running **ESCITW**. Not
corrupt, that goes without saying for **ESCITW**,
did u ever live in **ESCITW**? YEAH!
ESCITW has had its dirty laundry
something that could be said about **ESCITW**,
Venezuela, Australia and **ESCITW**. I ask you
How about the US pulls it military out of **ESCITW**
individual **ESCITW** is removable if the HO want. so an individual
community in **ESCITW** means absolutely nothing except
in Mexico, in Israel, in China, in Japan, in **ESCITW**
In **ESCITW**. And this true human and courageous
burma, just about **ESCITW** has got blood on its hands
but rather i think this culture war is between **ESCITW**
almost **ESCITW** today has borders which were
bad or boring restaurants in **ESCITW**) - and then
things in Thailand (and **ESCITW**) that are gennerally
like **ESCITW** as well, just not SOME people.
get to know **ESCITW**!
ESCITW has some tainted areas
I am not talking about **ESCITW** but when talking
I'd go to **ESCITW** *.* and I'd go to all of my friends
if we have managed to flourish in **ESCITW**
Poverty most exists in **ESCITW** even in Saudi Arabia
ESCITW ada MJ wanna be. Ada pertandingan tiru gaya dia

the greenest thing you can do is

is this: Choose the right leaders • **is** choose the right leaders • **is** use local materials • **is** make a house use less energy • **is** to not increase your lifestyle to go with money • **is** not to buy a hybrid car; it's to use a bicycle • **is** extend the life of what you already have • **is** to do nothing • **is** reduce the amount you use • **is** buy well made things that will last • **is** probably nothing at all, or much less of it • **is** vacation close to home • **is** design a building that somebody doesn't ever want to take down • **is** keep your computer out of the landfill • **is** nothing • **is** renovate a house • **is** to walk or cycle rather than use a car • **is** use public transport • **is** cut down on red meat altogether • **is** to minimize heat leaks • **is** use what you already have • **is** let your cat outside to do his business • **is** not build at all." • **is** a tight • **is** convert your lawn to a vegetable garden • **is** to choose the right people to lead our community • **is** to not build a new house, says Stan • **is** remodel the place you have • **is** tell them you just one your love • **is** to purchase a hy-brid or flex-fuel vehicle • **is** to extend the lifespan of the products you already own • **is** curb your consumption) • **is** keep your old car? • **is** to repair instead of buying new • **is** go out and spent $2K on area rugs • **is** not build the damned thing in the first place! • **is** use a facility that exists • **is** continue the life of an existing building • **is** to minimize heat leaks • **is** delay investing in any new appliance • **is** local, right. You know, people are into bamboo but • **is** research. Even Orbitz has an eco-friendly search function • **is** re-use! • **is** to not buy a computer at all • **is** remodel the place you have • **is** completely use something • **is** fucking kill yourself you ignorant • **is** to re-use an old building without gutting it • **is** keep the car you have, keep it in good condition • **is** reduce your footprint • **is** make a house use less energy • **is** to con-. tinue the life of an existing building • **is** not to have children • **is** make a house use less energy. Solar • **is** to attend your towns firework display • **is** to refrain from having babies • **is** not buy stuff you don't need • **is** to have no children. Any other act pales by comp • **is** keep your car • **is** to write, sing or speak about the movement for a sustainable • **is** cut it yourself. haha. what makes a haircut green • **is** not buy stuff you don't need • **is** keep an older car running • **is** keep a car on the road for as long as possible • **is** use things again.......and that's what antiquing is all about! • **is** to buy clothing that you then wear for years

your craziest relatives

Who are **your craziest relatives**? 1. I'm very close with my mother
preparing Thanksgiving dinner with **your craziest relatives** night, after night
inviting **your craziest relatives** along with you when you hit the town
your craziest relatives, a menagerie of exotic pets, and the neighbors
BETTER STEP ON YOUR TOES, CUZ IM ONE OF **your craziest relatives**
an alien in a Victorian picture frame and email it to **your craziest relatives**
kid could just as easily inherit the worst qualities of **your craziest relatives**
You tick 3 or 4 of **your craziest relatives** off and THEY have you committed

why my dog always

tell me **why my dog always** barks when someone comes in
Why is **my dog always** rubbing his butt on the floor?

I'm wondering **why my dog always** stinks so bad
anyone know **why my dog always** smells really bad?

I understand **why my dog always** barks
Why my dog always struggle when I hold on
I would ask **why my dog always** sniff other peoples
Why? My dog always has his collar on

I always wondered **why my dog always** got mad when
I wonder if that's **why my dog always** picked this one
maybe that is **why my dog always** salivated

I know **why my dog always** has so much fun while I am
wondering **why my dog always** runs to the door when
I know **why my dog always** raises his leg at the brand new

I don't get **why my dog always** appear in my photos
I wish I understood **why my dog always** does & & &

In any case, this is **why my dog always** knows
why my dog always drags its ass
why my dog always splashes her paws about
Why My Dog Always Spill Of The Water I Give Him
Why My Dog Always Bite Me
I now understand **why my dog always** splashes

tell me **why my dog always** hang out on the couch
Why my dog always flu?

That explains **why my dog always** gets them things
why my dog always has to get into the garbage
why my dog always mumble, but my dog like to play
couldn't figure out **why my dog always** smelled

tell me **why my dog always** goes toilet in the house
why-my-dog-always-goes-garden-pass-urine
Why my dog always get a cough and never stop?
I wonder **why my dog always** barks always barks
I don't know **why my dog always** shake

possible reason **why my dog always** sneezes on me
why my dog always got mad when I went to Disneyland
that's **why my dog always** wants to have sex with the neighbor
why my dog always had the urge to lick himself when
sounds like $\sum$ **why my dog always**

i wear something red

on Valentines day, shall **i wear something red** or another colour ?
Should **I wear something red** or is that too matchy?
Everytime **I wear something red**, I get compliments. But
only for night time when **I wear something red**. Brands
need to make sure **I wear something red** every day to ward off the negative

when **I wear something red**. It seems to go with anything. I also
when **I wear something red** I wear red long earrings
If **I wear something Red** Sox, a Yankees fan cannot -- I mean
should **I wear? Something red**?' 'Mmmm, maybe, but keep it
cool! i make sure **i wear something red** everyday!

The problem with blue is if **I wear something red**, then
I wear something red when I have a meeting that is predominantly
the evil-eye and that if **i wear something red** or ared tring i will
I WEAR SOMETHING RED OR BLACK OR BOTH EVERYDAY.
If **I wear something red**, it will make me active

I wear something red every day. My favorite number is 3.
I wear something red. I believe red brings us luck. While mom
my mum INSISTS **I wear something red**... I guess I could.
Chinese saying,i will be unlucky unless **i wear something red**,such as
When I feel like I need to be brave, **I wear something red**

I wear something red at all times - wards off the evil eye
every time **I wear something red** near my face, I try to do that
feeling "pretty" man gud ko if **I wear something red**....charrrrrr!
Say for example, **I wear something red** for my birthday since
In honor of JC **I wear something red** on the 22nd of every month

if fish could talk they

18/19

IF FISH COULD TALK THEY WOULD SAY: 'Just keep swimming
If fish could talk they no doubt would tell enlightening tales of passage
if fish could talk, they would probably be telling us some very important things

If fish could talk, they would probably ask for Tetra. Made from the finest
If fish could talk, they'd probably tell you that the dirty water needs to be cleaned
If fish could talk, they'd shriek with pleasure when his/her dirty old tank becomes

Yes, but perhaps if fish could talk they would tell you they don't give a hoot

If fish could talk...they'd sound like whales
If fish could talk they'd say 'You guys are killing us'
If fish could talk, they would judge all fishermen to be evil
If fish could talk, they wouldn't

If fish could talk, they'd say "thanks" for Feed-Air
And if fish could talk, they'd say "EAT MORE BEEF!"
If fish could talk, they would probably ask for Bio-Superior (F)
if fish could talk, they probably would not have a word for water

If fish could talk they would wave
If fish could talk, they would warn

bail out I said

bail out i said

He insisted that they should be a **bail out. I said**
he asked if we wanted to **bail out. I said**
talking about a **bail out. I said** deregulation caused these problems

on the green or in the water, no place to **bail out. I said**
these securities have no choice but to **bail out. I said**
When the City was gagging for a **bail-out, I said** he
advised me to **bail out. I said**, ‚Not over enemy territory.‘

word came back from P-38 pilots that they couldn't **bail out. I said**,
that's when I had to **bail out. I said**, „This is not about me
operator and pilot came back and said we were to **bail out. I said**
I told you it wasn't a real **bail-out. I said** on Friday
If there's a 700 billion **bail out.... i said**
and, while speaking about the **bail-out I said**

the minute they announced the Fannie and Freddie **bail-out, I said**
Don't **bail out,“ I said**. „Don't bail out
associates pressed him to **bail out. „I said**, ‚No. Four years from now
and after my last **bail out, I said** I would never go back

they were going to but then they would **bail out. I said** i was going
to the bomb line where he told me to **bail out. I said**, Naw, I'll get her back
The crew said `can we **bail out?‘ I said** `hell no‘
Bail out I said bail out

75

i knew was trouble

allowing someone else to pick up a domain **I knew was trouble**
One of the kids, who **I knew was trouble**, walked up to me
which **I knew was trouble** . I must digress here
but this **I knew was trouble**
to go some place or do something that **I knew was trouble**

The one time I dated someone **I knew was trouble**
his plane started to move in a strange slow motion that **I knew was trouble**
speeds by which **I knew was trouble** already because I could see

I knew was trouble in the funnest form
saying stupid stinkin' kicker **I knew was trouble** from the start
a girl who **I knew was trouble**. When I asked him
She gave the lady the look **I knew was trouble**
So I started hanging out with this girl who **I knew was trouble**
just a 'need to refresh' button which **I knew was trouble**

all of my money in a

a particular index • **a** single location • **a** CD for a year • **a** chain of Amy Winehouse hair salons • **a** CD with a growth rate of just barely higher than inflation • **a** company that most think is more likely than not to go bankrupt • **a** bad investment • **a** mutual fund at T. Rowe Price • **a** debit card in china • **a** high interest checking account • **a** matter of hours • **a** savings account and checking account • **a** bank invest it where it can bring in more money • **a** factory business with a treacherous team • **a** savings account • **a** simple jar, all $5.80 worth • **a** game of poker in West Yellowstone • **a** pro studio • **a** portfolio which is growing each day • **a** stock market reversal or a bad commodity • **a** few hours mostly all to one player • **a** life annuity, will there be anything left for my kids? • **a** mutual fund? • **a** bath tub and sit in it • **a** bag and hide it in my letters • **a** CD account and into stock • **a** store like this. Things I need • **a** sub account which cannot be accessed by others • **a** company that produces toxic waste for Eastern European movie sets • **a** sock in the yard • **a** blind trust until I complete my probation • **a** cash lump sum payment today • **a** hurry • **a** Dixie cup in my room! • **a** mattress • **a** country that apparently doesn't want honestly want me • **a** plutonium mine in Chile, for example • **a** big brown bag inside a zoo • **a** single stock • **a** wallet • **a** secret location (the trunk of my car) • **a** bond yielding me 5% annually • **a** brutal game of Stratego the night before • **A** YEAR!!! srry. (dont like to brag) • **a** precious-metals fund • **a** Nigerian bank account • **a** Freedom bank account in Zurich • **a** day or so! • **a** foreign country one night • **a** refrigerator like Rep. William Jefferson • **a** poker game. Payday was four days away

how much i bought into

I didn't realize **how much I bought into** this stereotype
how much I bought into the bubble way of life

I'm just amazed at **how much I bought into** that wasn't
how much I bought into what our culture teaches

showed me **how much I bought into** Yankee myths
how much I bought into all the warnings about marriage

black and white I saw the world and **how much I bought into**
and **how much I bought into** the hype beforehand

how much I bought into this idea of such a skilled liar
about most things, so I don't know **how much I bought into** into

how much I bought into this form of negative thinking, until
I just can't believe **how much I bought into** that, and it seems

I am astonished at **how much I bought into** it
how much I bought into the idea about having the perfect bod

I don't know **how much I bought into** that before May
how much I bought into being selfless

I don't know **how much I bought into** the idea
I remember **how much I bought into** the hype

I'm amazed at **how much I bought into** it
just **how much I bought into** the illusion of Celebrity

how much I bought into the right-wing nutjob super fundament
how much I bought into his remarks or how much

how much I bought into the story to the extent that I was totally
out of my control, no matter **how much I bought into** diet culture

how much I bought into it myself like Pinocchio
how much I bought into the Fruit Roll-Up scene

how much I bought into his lonely, socially-awkward murder
when i think **how much i bought into** the hype a few years ago

only seen it once -- but I was amazed at **how much I bought into** it
how much I had been spoon fed and **how much I bought into**,

didn't recall **HOW much I bought into** Jaime's story until I read
how invested into the world/**how much I bought into** its values

how much I bought into it. This is a story unto itself
how much I bought into the hype of this latest release

so out of control for so long

so out of control for so long that he's fucking going blind
I felt **so out of control for so long** that it seemed hopeless
I was **so out of control for so long** that the Chaos of living life while
Manhattan has been **so out of control for so long**
cheating has been **so out of control for so long**
letting this (New York) situation get **so out of control for so long**

the LAX team has been **so out of control for so long**
I just felt **so out of control for so long**
been **so out of control for so long**, my body has been dehydrated
our eating habits have been **so out of control for so long**
being **so out of control for so long** and melting into violence is NOT normal
After my blood sugars being **so out of control for so long**

I have never been **so out of control for so long**
Olympia has been **so out of control for so long**
father had let things get **so out of control for so long**
don't understand why her situation has been **so „out of control" for so long**!
my life had been **so out of control for so long** that this was possibly
When they come to us their lives have been **so out of control for so long**

because the police department was **so out of control for so long**
Blood in semen sugar control after being **so out of control for so long**?
I can't believe that I was **so out of control for so long**
Our Government has been **so out of control for so long**
so titanically complex, and has been **so out of control for so long**
suffering its effects now (because it's been **so out of control for so long**)

but i was so hungry i could

9/9

but I was so hungry I could hardly wait
but I was so hungry I could have eaten a horse
it was good but I was so hungry, I could have eaten anything

but I was so hungry I could have eaten an entire field's worth of sun
You can add lettuce but I was so hungry I could not wait
but I was so hungry I could not concentrate

The berries were bitter but I was so hungry I could not stop
But i was so hungry I could not bother to re-heat it
But I was so hungry, I could hardly carry my. daughter

just because you never know if

just because you never know if you hit a person or not
just because you never know if you'd need it
just because you never know if there will be a good one

Just because you never know if life is gonna toss you a bone
just because you never know if you are able to catch the bus you want
just because you never know if you are going combat maces someday

just because you never know if the scar is going to form
just because you never know if someone is going to have something
just because you never know if it is going to work out

just because you never know if someone will or not
just because. You never know if someone will want it
Just because you never know if they have something going on

just because you never know if the other guys are going to hit some threes
just because you never know if you will regret it
just because you never know if somethings going to happen

that was the second i

That **was the second** I became a surfer
that was the second i knew that computer games are going to
and **that was the second** I closed the book
That was the second I was waiting. for.
That was the second I started realizing 2000 miles away that Gramma still rules

in front of the queen! **that was the second** I knew that he,s out of the band)
because **that was the second** I saw the car
that was the start, **that was the second** I made up my mind
That was the second. I got my scuba
so I guess **that was the second.** I just asked him to show me

so **that was the second.i** thought i die that time
that was the second. I may have been rejected
I totally knew what **that was the second** I saw it. My mom is a bird fanatic.
one Amendment in the entire bleeding Bill of Rights and **that was the Second? I**
that was the second. i wasnt there the first time

that was the second i became interested in animals
I think **that was the second.** I,d probably read another.
you dropped it. **that was the second i** realized that it was everything but
wasn,t good enough for her, and **that was the second.** I had NO idea
That was the second I decided I wanted to become an actor

That was the second -- I think I spoke to him only three
That was the second, I think. Maybe the third
that was the second i cried
Or maybe **that was the second.** I think maybe the first was the plumb
and **that was the second i** realized i wanted to mary this man

not even for a million dollars would i

12/12

not even for a million dollars Would I ever want to let you go
Not even for a million dollars, would I agree
not even for a million dollars would i do that
not even for a million dollars would I swap them for one instant
Not even for a million dollars would I so much step on board one
Not even for a million dollars would I shag him
not even for a million dollars would I ever leave here
Not even for a million dollars would I ask someone to do that
Not even for a million dollars would I jump
Not even for a million dollars would I commit those errors again
not even for a million dollars would I be party to any bullshit busts for same
Not even for a million dollars would I take your DISOBEDIENT DUMBASS BACK!

if i had a million dollars
the first thing i would do
11/11

if i had a million dollars the first thing i would do is buy a car

If I had a million dollars the first thing I would do would be to pay off my house

If I had a million dollars the first thing I would do would be: hire assistant coach

If I had a million dollars the first thing I would do with it I would buy a nice

If I had a million dollars. the first thing I would do would be pay off my parents'

If I had a million dollars, the first thing I would do is pay off the mortgages

if i had a million dollars, the first thing i would do is complete my gilmore girls

If I had a million dollars, the FIRST thing I would do is set up a trust fund for my

if I had a million dollars, the first thing I would do is get out of here

if I had a million dollars, the first thing I would do, after paying tithing, would be

If I had a million dollars the first thing I would do is fly around the world and see

systems tugging

13/13

hundreds of **systems tugging** at our every thought and deed
the weight of several handheld gaming **systems tugging** at your pants
in linear **systems: Tugging** a rope attached to a wagon causes
Source Level **Systems Tugging** Scrubbing Participate matter clogs
finally result in six or seven **systems tugging** at the boy saying,
(1) we identified two major competing value **systems tugging** on our
solar **systems, tugging** entire groups of planets across galaxies,
two irreconcilable **systems tugging** at the fundamental
battle that's faced when there are multiple belief **systems tugging**
belief **systems tugging** and churning and merging and
many incentive **systems tugging** away at the same resources
opponent **systems tugging** away at each other in their brains,
on the came and my **systems. Tugging**

what does priceless mean

what does priceless mean? what is the meaning of priceless?
what does priceless mean? what is the definition for priceless?
Meaning of priceless . **What does priceless mean**? Proper usage and pronunciation
What does priceless mean? Information and translations of priceless
Another word for priceless **What does priceless mean**?

What does priceless mean? „ Why did the king think the cats were priceless?"
What does priceless mean? „ Why did the king think he had given Luigi a
priceless gift?" **What does „priceless" mean**? Is anything really „priceless"?
what does „priceless" mean? Bob thinks of old movies
What does priceless mean? (so valuable that no price is high enough

Dad, **what does „priceless" mean**?
what does priceless mean????? happy
What does priceless mean? tried to smash. a porcelain Madonna
what does priceless mean? by Ollla - Your English Dictionary
priceless (**what does priceless mean**?) precious (what does precious mean?)

after long thought i decided

30/30

After long thought, I decided to attend
After long thought, I decided to just call

After long thought, I decided that it would be better to stay
After long thought, I decided to approach

After long thought I decided on my knowledge of human nature
after long thought I decided it was from my peers

But after long thought I decided to have another go at it
After long thought, I decided that I was so anxious

after long thought i decided ive had enough of your
After long thought I decided I would go

After long thought I decided to breed this shrimp as I wanted
After long thought, I decided this blog belongs to me

After long thought I decided I must abide to her
after long thought, I decided that my vote

after long thought i decided to come into the fold of socialest party
and finally, after long thought I decided to get a sniper

After long thought, I decided to follow the masses
After long thought, I decided on, of all. places, Hawaii

after long thought- I decided that smelling like garlic wasn't as bad as
After long thought, I decided that I'd sacrifice

After long thought, I decided I would engrave his to say
After long thought, I decided to import the old blog over

Today, **after long thought, I decided** to renew my life
Soooo..... **after long thought I decided** to get out my surger

After long thought, I decided that insane blogging might be amusing
after long thought I decided that no huns were going to determine

After long thought, I decided to supplement the written text
After long thought I decided I really didn't like it

After long thought, I decided to play
after long thought I decided that nobody's opinion of me will sensor what I

as for how to help

As for how to help, I would say keep your ears open
As for how to help others, there are many ways
As for how to help your husband, my suggestion is

As for how to help us NOW: The biggest way
As for how to help describe your feelings, I find
As for how to help your damaged hair, the first thing

As for how to help with the nausea, I've heard that gin
As for how to help, my best advice is to just reassure her
As for how to help her, I really wouldn't know

As for how to help introduce it from the bottom up
but **as for how to help**, my friend just had a baby
and **as for how to help** you deal with it?Your either going to

As for how to help John: 1. He's got to want help
As for how to help him, I don't think you can. except
Given that he is an adult your options **as for how to help**

As for how to help children with it, make sure they socialize
As for how to help her you may try compiling the advice
As for how to help support your hubby, just talk to him

As for how to help, Mongabay had a really great
As for how to help people bear those costs, I'm not sure
As for how to help, ask Attorney Bill

as for how to help her get ready -- just be supportive
As for how to help you.. i'd most likely need to see
a loss **as for how to help**? This is the web-site for you

As for how to help your child choose a college,
As for how to help them, it beats me. Should they
just do that.. **as for how to help** them not get

As for how to help with the show, "!"s renewal
As for how to help put it together? I have absolutely no idea
As for how to help them out on the road, I'm not sure

As for how to help the 47 million; create more jobs
As for how to help the services reduce bike fatalities,
As for how to help the cause with a donation you can

As for how to help the poor on site: the Dutch do it
As for how to help you, you should talk to a psychologist
as for how to help your friend, I would tell her

good or bad.39 **As for how to help** strengthen
As for how to help your first child through
As for how to help protect your computer.... Well,

As for how to help Ohloh, I'm not sure how to help
I feel a bit tied up **as for how to help** my people
as for how to help. Now that I'm here

this ginormous cloud

this ginormous cloud

and we looked over and **this ginormous cloud** of birds raised up into the
this ginormous cloud that looked so surreal b/c it had so much depth and
makes **this GINORMOUS cloud** of tiny fizzy bubbles
at Cape Erimo, Hokkaido, Japan with **this ginormous cloud**
because my neighbors started looking outside to see **this ginormous cloud**
went to open the blinds and there was **this ginormous cloud** covering

this ginormous cloud of smoke coming rushing my way. So i
have **this ginormous cloud** of social guilt that I've been carrying
under **this ginormous cloud** of smoke. Like we are living on
this GINORMOUS cloud in the distance. It's pretty
how the weather shows **this ginormous cloud**. Hehehehehe, oh the
fire over Thanksgiving break produced **this ginormous cloud**

on the other side of the Altamont Pass, **this ginormous cloud**
this ginormous cloud almost right above my house, and it was
outside waving me off and the boxster farts **this ginormous cloud** of
silver lining in **this ginormous cloud** is knowing that there are people
there.... we passed **this ginormous cloud** cloud
this ginormous cloud just floated over

more than ones and zeros

physically nothing **more than ones and zeros**
stored as nothing **more than ones and zeros**
made of **more than ones and zeros**;
Life is so much **more than ones and zeros**
something composed of **more than ones and zeros**

multifaceted humanity through little **more than ones and zeros**
unique traits in that they manipulate **more than ones and zeros**
worlds are nothing **more than ones and zeros** doesn't mean they aren't
more than ones and zeros. Mark Spencer Mark Spencer is President

Difference: **more than ones and zeros**. We deliver
more than ones and zeros. 6. Future Work. This paper has
more than ones and zeros, encoded as plus or minus

Networking today is about **more than ones and zeros**
the end of the day is really nothing **more than ones and zeros**

nothing **more than ones and zeros**. your tv then has to accept
more than ones and zeros as a person has to come up with a way

Life is **more than ones and zeros**, and
Your kitchen spoon is nothing **more than ones and zeros**
more than ones and zeros, cannot be shared, cannot be sold

what the FDIC claimed as "assets" were no **more than ones and zeros**,
more than ones and zeros!

but for anyone who desires a little **more than ones and zeros**,
when text and photos are nothing **more than ones and zeros** forever
more than ones and zeros passing me by
nothing **more than ones and zeros**. Organic
and even cold, hard, raw data is **more than ones and zeros**

printed money is nothing **more than ones and zeros** in a computer
they are nothing **more than ones and zeros** on the hard drive
for artists..musicians need to become **more than ones and zeros**
more than ones and zeros in a document file: it's the lifeblood
spreadsheet: **more than ones and zeros**

Armed with nothing **more than ones and zeros**,
essentially nothing **more than ones and zeros**, but yet
supossedly passing nothing **more than ones and zeros** that
sees them as nothing **more than ones and zeros**
mail is worth infinitely **more than ones and zeros**

To it, your guitar is nothing **more than ones and zeros**. Further
systems working with **more than ones and zeros** would just need

People are **more than ones and zeros**." "What?

What exists in electronic form is nothing **more than ones and zeros**
and her hand fades through the screen as nothing **more than ones and zeros**

and oprah invited

and **Oprah invited** die-hard Sex and the City fans
and **Oprah invited** you and me. I'm so grateful
to make the drive home, **and Oprah invited** her to

blog about the show . . . **and Oprah invited** me up on stage!
and Oprah invited 1000 fans to Chicago
and Oprah invited her to be on the show!

and Oprah invited Chris Rock to share scenes from
YouTube **and Oprah invited** him to present it on her show
and Oprah invited her

and Oprah invited him, remember--awesome,
The two became good friends, **and Oprah invited** him
and Oprah invited me to her show

and Oprah invited Alexie to appear on her show
and Oprah invited some rappers
and Oprah invited her to give the viewers her advice on

Larry King **and Oprah invited** him to join them
by sending an e-mail, **and Oprah invited** him
and Oprah invited the actors from the movie

They went home **and Oprah invited** Reggie to help
Charice **and Oprah invited** her. The rest is history
And Oprah invited the women Dove featured in their ads on her TV

whenever tom cruise is

First Rule: drink **whenever Tom Cruise is** a slick bastard
Whenever Tom Cruise is slighted he can just say, "Hey!
Whenever Tom Cruise is mentioned in an interview with someone
whenever Tom Cruise is written about, it always says he is a Scientologist
Whenever Tom Cruise is reported to have a new girlfriend, I tell my wife, "Hey,
whenever Tom Cruise is around, L Ron Hubbard never is
And she will supposedly "give birth" **whenever Tom Cruise is** ready

my personal american idol

She's **my personal American idol**," said Doolittle. "I was in heaven
the fabulousness of Jobriath, **my personal American Idol**. My
patrick(**MY personal american idol**) pictures from
Adam Lambert is **My Personal American Idol**.

My personal American Idol, Adam Lambert did a stint as fashion reporter for
My personal American Idol, John Ford, saw Earp as a key American archtype.
"The Chosen One" - so befitting **my personal American Idol** of Season 7,
my personal American Idol, DIDI Benami leaves this season.

Added to. Quicklist0:11 $\sum$ **my personal american idol**. 113 views.

about judging new voices like its **my personal American Idol**
My personal American Idol is now officially America's Idol.
What was up with **MY personal American Idol**, Michael Johns,
I told him ,"No I have not met **my personal american idol**: Dr. Barry Maron
is "Strictly Genteel", which covers the work of **my personal American Idol** from
my personal "American Idol". GOD Bless You MSG DeLuca.

This is **my personal American Idol** final. I want this job. In other news,
You are **my personal American Idol**, no matter what happens.

My Personal American Idol. January 30, 2007 $\sum$ Leave a Comment.

Zac Efron Secretly Loves Me. !ê **My Personal American Idol**
Johnny Weir, **my personal American idol** ladies and gentlemen. Really,
2 years in a row **my personal American Idol** favorite won and
My personal American Idol should have the following: GOD

My personal American Idol Highlight: Simon might be right:
ELVIS will always be **my personal, American Idol** !!!! Its just sorta fun
how's it feels to be **my PERSONAL American Idol**

My Personal American Idol My little boy loves to sing,
I was lucky enough to meet **my personal American Idol**, Carrie
Such a sad, sad day for me as **my personal American Idol**, DIDI
My personal American idol, Barbra Streisand, has credited
Jasmine because La Toya (**my personal American Idol**) got

Full Version: **My Personal American Idol** Thread ∑ Doghouse Boxing
My Personal American Idol Thread. Track this topic | Email
Read **My personal American Idol** Highlights Season 5 by S
MacArthur indeed is **my personal American Idol**!
My personal American Idol is and will always be Tasia!

∑ Early Evening Pick Me Up ∑ **My Personal American Idol**
My Personal American Idol ∑ The Way of the Future

the chance tonight to hang out with **my personal american idol** ACE YOUNG!
But, he is not **my personal American Idol** choice because what makes
My Personal American Idol History.

My Personal American Idol Top 12 for Season 8: Adam Lambert
and he has talent. **My personal American Idol** is Elliot.
For the first time in **my personal American Idol** history,
Adam Lambert is **My Personal American Idol**. of this document.

you are **my personal american idol**, hehehehe!
call me for a little session of **my personal American Idol**

i this i that

"i" this "i" that "i pod" "i phone" "i tampon"
it's always about "me" or I this I that

I this- I that- I want- I need
I-this, I-that, I-wanna-access-facebook-from-my-phone,
I this, I that, I the other.. Think of another f**kin

sucks at socializing'-'I this..I that'.I think it took
I this, I that, I, I, I. As if I was all that mattered

stop that 'I this, I that, I, I, I. On the contrary,
I glad, I this I that , I vex because no one
available to us , and I this, I that, I, I, I,
I this... I that... I me mine... Which can be a bit
I want, I hurt, I this, I that, I everything."

start with I-this, I-that. "I" seems content to
I this I that. I hate I like I enjoy I love I want
I'm using the word "I" this, "I" that, "I" the other
I this. I that. I blah. I yadda. Try something more
self-involved, everything is i-this, i-that, i, me, and
I this, I that, I the other thing. I get tired of seeing
I this, I that, I...I...I...I . Six I = Self absorbed.

I this I that I then I.......goes on and on!
I that I am and I this I that I am
I this, I that, I this, I that, I this .... I, I, I,
All I see in your posts is I this, I that, I would, I love
i this i that i c..ck ˘ i va....ina.....i everything

And that`s the word "I." **"I" this, "I" that**,
I snorted; **I this, I that**. I didn't inject. But
I this / I that / I think this / I did that /
I this. I that. I'm doing my best to get you textbooks.

I this I that I, I , I ME ME ME. MMM Mmm Mmm
I this, I that, I, I, I, all the time, the focus of the
self without resorting to **I this, I that**, I the other, I, I, I?
 ... **I this... I that**... I, I, I. It was a behind the scene look at
God by saying I first, **I this, I that**, I heard

I This, I That, I Talk About Myself
I this,.....I that,....I am.....that I am......! Bull **it!
I This, I That, I The Other..." This is not a female thing,
I that, **I this, I that** and they actually most of the time don't
get their I's tested: **I THIS , I THAT** , I
just write **I this, I that**, I usually fail to read beyond

Not **I this, I that**, I believe
i organize, i sew, **i this, i that**, i.... i collect
"**I this I that** i chat whether i pod or i mac

kicking in, u know, **I this, I that**, I think this, I think that
"**i this i that**, i everything." - Apple iPad (16GB) user review and

"I" this, "I" that, "I" everything. That is well and fine but
Every single sentence read, "**I this, I that**, I am, I can...
i this i that i everywhere

mcluhan and warhol

McLuhan and Warhol inhabit a certain pop sensibility
Conditioned by **McLuhan and Warhol**, Johnny Carson and Phil Donahue,
From **McLuhan and Warhol** to USA Today,
in the ideas of **McLuhan and Warhol** and the post-modernists

here Benjamin preempts both **McLuhan and Warhol** in formulating
a perfect manifestation of what **McLuhan and Warhol** augured
in different epochs by Orwell, **McLuhan, and Warhol**,
by **McLuhan and Warhol**: wanting a poetry that will 'reach people'

that **McLuhan and Warhol** are related on their views about art
is whatever you can get away with" is attributed to both **McLuhan and Warhol**
I was tuned in to **McLuhan and Warhol** early on and realized
I'm a big fan of Marshall **McLuhan and Warhol** and stuff

the predictions of **McLuhan and Warhol** that ring ever truer in
McLuhan and Warhol. Some of his stunts include
a perfect manifestation of what **McLuhan and Warhol** augured
McLuhan and Warhol have love

ever since i joined facebook

ever since I joined facebook, many, many months ago
Ever since I joined Facebook a few years ago I have been telling friends
Ever since I joined Facebook in July 2007, I've been an evangelist
My problem: Ever since I joined Facebook in July, it has always been "balky."

At first i was into myspace, but ever since i joined facebook
ever since i joined facebook, the junk never stops coming
Ever since I joined Facebook I have been amazed and curious

Ever since I joined Facebook, I have NOT asked any hot woman
for probably only the second time ever since I joined facebook

ever since I joined Facebook (I think it was around 2004) I've been a lot better
My life's gotten a little too full ever since i joined facebook
communicating with people on-line ever since i joined "Facebook"
getting steadily worse ever since I joined Facebook last summer
Ever since I joined Facebook in June, I've become an excellent stalker

Sorry, ever since I joined facebook i've been neglecting my
Ever since I joined facebook, I don't even log on

Ever since I joined Facebook this summer, I haven't been able to
ever since i joined facebook I kind of stopped

Ever since I joined Facebook and started this blog, I have been reconnecting
wala na akong activity sa Friendster ever since I joined Facebook
But, ever since I joined Facebook and reconnected with so many old friends
Ever since I joined Facebook, I have come across names

clicked on god

I **clicked on God** Made The Trees and I found
when I **clicked on God** speaks through the intercessors,
I mistakenly **clicked on God** and smote Him.
I played for over 30 minutes, and **clicked on god** knows how much
for some odd reason I **clicked on God** of Study and guess what?
(**clicked on God** of War 3 and Uncharted 2) just to see
when I **clicked on "God** Only Knows," my very first thought

I **clicked on "God** Loves A Drunk" (2nd link) expecting
I first **clicked on "God"**, and was sad to see
I just ramdomly **clicked on God** is love's page, and saw
LE PLAYER, in the title of the thread you **clicked on god**
wasnt a big deal, only a little joke, but when i **clicked on god**
to take care of them eaiser. I **clicked on "God"** the pokemon so
for the love of god" when i **clicked on "god"**

my daughter **clicked on god** knows what and it shut me down
I **clicked on god** knows what and all my toolbars and all my icons
until i **clicked on "God** wants you to know"
When I **clicked on God@God.com**
and **clicked on god** of war like 30 times like and
clicked on god almighty's pic. Me and him laughed
and **clicked on "God"** - one of the tags in "My Interests" -

thankyou!!! That did it. I must have **clicked on god**
clicked on god knows what (miscellaneous) and
having **clicked on god** knows how many annoying links
when the light **clicked on; god**, he'd forgotten how bright
So I **clicked on God** under my Technorati tags
clicked on god-knows how many malicious links on websites
this is the 8 channel i **clicked on! GOD!!!!!!!!!!** lol random

finally a video that proves

10/10

Finally a video that proves the existence of ghosts
Finally! A video that proves the occult has infiltrated Christian rock
finally, a video that proves i wasnt crazy
Finally, a video that proves Global Warming
Finally a video that proves str hybrids do about the same damage as pure str
Finally, a video that proves that John Travolta was the best Muppet
Finally a video that proves that Cambodia use to own most of southeast Asia
We all know this guy at the party. **Finally a video that proves** his motives
half the building still standing after the initial collapse. **Finally a video that proves**
Walks on F&?kin water, No shit!!! Ok **finally, a video that proves** it

no tv never

No TV: **never** did me any harm
after close to 90 days still **no TV. NEVER** purchase a
social life - and I have **no TV. Never** found the need
to screw the customer.. still **no TV... NEVER** BUY
NO Tv, never have. Both of our parents also
then called Dish and canceled. **No TV, never** been happier.

I have **no tv, never** go to the cinema
with the same meal 3 times a day, **no tv, never**
No TV. Never. No TV. Another tea. Day 2.

Buddy knows he's on cruise, **no T.V., never** hears
the Illinois river, got internet but **no TV. Never** assume
connection to the modern world: he has **no TV, never** goes
no TV, never have. I am retired--get most of my serious info
surfing the net at work! No idea - **no TV, never** seen the squarepants.

always a debate of TV vs. **no TV, never** animation vs. reality

No car, **no TV. Never** even used tubes and buses
the past few weeks - **no TV (never** had

Have **no TV? Never** seen many photographs on magazines?
that most certainly means no or almost **no TV. Never**
live under a rock...with **no TV...never** reading anything about
no tv, never had it. The pc, which I use for studies belongs
to this strand or soon ther'll be **no TV (never** mind cctv), cars,
card was debited, **no TV (never** even been in stock)

Before anyone asks: nope, **no TV, never** needed one
No TV. Never complained." White wasn't complaining
I haven't heard it (I have **no TV, never** thought I'd be
seriously - **no tv - never** listen to radio or get much news

just a woodstove, **no TV, never** knowing
no heating, **no tv, never** cleaned in 7 days,
seen the view, another perk to **no TV. Never** thought
cable was out!!!! **NO TV! Never** AGAIN!

No, TV never bores me, but it always interests me

No tv, never. Under our bedrooms there's
no idea who he is. (**No TV, never** saw an episode
in fact we had **no tv! never** danced, went to
nature's rhythms, watching **no TV, never** seeing anything
Spontaneous - **No TV/never** watches TV now, 1, 0
maybe **no TV.... never** mind la... got laptop maybe

leave that machine alone

Why can't just **leave that machine alone**. Still have to spent
slot etiquette teaches that you should **leave that machine alone**

you might as well **leave that machine alone**, and start from scratch
leave that machine alone! You might get hurt if you touch it

I pretty much **leave that machine alone**, so it's locked
If not, let's **leave that machine alone** 'til we get machine #1 clean

He just /couldn't/ **leave that machine alone** for long, could he ? LOL !
The time machine   I think I would **leave that machine alone**

you want to **leave that machine alone** when it is printing
I had to **leave that machine alone** for a few days----I didn't

affect this (I usually **leave that machine alone**!
start this and **leave that machine alone** until it is done. I

think I'll **leave that machine alone** from now on. Thanks for the input
I was going to **leave that machine alone** and use the TV Pack one

I was just gonna **leave that machine alone** while I had the SR open
and you should be very happy **leave that machine alone** until

we decide it's best to just **leave that machine alone**,
Today it will be ,"don;t you ever **leave that machine alone**?

to all the people who are saying "just l**leave that machine alone!!**"
Might have to **leave that machine alone** for now, or use it

Armstrong, I thought I told you to **leave that machine alone**."
[Cor'non]: **leave that machine alone**! While fighting

you need **leave that machine alone** ... the individual runtimes
want a coasterless burn consistently, why not just **leave that machine alone**?

Leave that machine alone till I get back. What'd you do to it.
Leave that machine alone till I get back. What'd you do to it?

Leave that machine alone!, 6 Di que sì
unfortunatly they are not us, so we just **leave that machine alone** :(

May I also suggest that you physically (entirely) **leave that machine alone**
Leave that machine alone! Oh Jill, the cat conversation is

to delete a bunch of stuff, then **leave that machine alone** for an hour and
Leave that machine alone. R+x∞ê£S⌷g:

after I told them to **leave that machine alone**, my 9 month old daughter
recommend you **leave that machine alone** and save for a new one

which made it ideal when I needed to **leave that machine alone**
leave that machine alone I think because it's scaring the hell out of

as we all emerge

the creature made me

the creature made me get fired

The creature made me do it!

the Creature made me almost want to take him in my arms

the creature made me think

the creature made me fall in love

The creature made me promise to send one of you to the castle

the creature made me envious, he touched it so admirably

you need on this earth

9/9

The last thing **you need on this earth** is a LIBERAL ACCOUNTANT
I hope i will be all **you need on this earth**
Don,t you even know what **you need on this earth**?

Is all that **you need on this earth**
God has equipped you to have everything **you need on this earth**
the last thing **you need on this Earth** is a sudden deviation in power

Having all the money **you need on this earth** is merely having
the last thing **you need on this earth**--a coffin
Sometimes the freedom is not the only thing **you need on this earth**

if you humans would

11/11

Well, **if you humans would** learn to clean up your toys
If you humans would consider the magnitude of your past guilt
And **if you humans would** only ever consider the suffering you have to endure
If you humans would eat a few of your kids here 'n there

be so much easier **if you humans would** just put out a small pile of grain
we would really appreciate it **if you humans would** stop
It would serve us all **if you humans would** remember the rest of us

If you humans would watch our TV commercials you would know
If you humans would just follow our lead
if you humans would just call Pooch Sitter, I'm sure
a nice functional place that can take care of itself **if you humans would**

do i really look like i need

Do I really look like I need one?

do I really look like I need 2 get drunk
Do I REALLY look like I need to lose ten pounds

do I really look like I need to be told to "hang in there"?
Do I really look like I need to work?? Hi Guys!
god people...do i really look like i need this right now?

Do I really look like I need your money?
Do I really look like I need the shoes
Do I really look like I need the help?!
I'm dining alone, do I really look like I need to tie-one-on?
Do I really look like I need to be told another story?

Do I really look like I need saving? What were you thinking?
do i really look like i need that much help?
Do I really look like I need five hundred dollars?
Do I really look like I need to be saved that much?
do I really look like I need it? I guess so hahas. Hmmm
but then again - do I really look like I need early intervention?

totally hilarious that you

I think it **totally hilarious that you** chose to delete my comment
totally hilarious that you changed it to d-pom
completly and **totally hilarious that you**'re moving in
totally hilarious that you're still trying to defend them
totally hilarious that you had a cup on your computer
haha I think its **totally hilarious that you** think I'm a white boy
and **totally hilarious that you** go from that narrow-minded perspective to
find it **totally hilarious that you** all have nothing better to do then complain
totally hilarious that you say this, of all things
it's **totally hilarious that you** look the way you do
It is **totally hilarious that you** got spammed for lonliness
so **totally hilarious that you** will just have to leave in disgust
totally hilarious that you're able to dress
its **totally hilarious that you** listed the name
totally hilarious that you're touting evidence around which disproves your theories
It's also **totally hilarious that you** would register through the discovery channel
totally hilarious that you still stand by such ceasefires and accords
I think it is **totally HILARIOUS that you** can watch the road
totally hilarious that you cannot find a single this about the candidate HIMSELF
Totally hilarious that you global warming deniers are taking up this art
something **totally hilarious that you** find absolutely fitting
totally hilarious that you didn't spell „dictionary.com" correctly.

when i see a windmill

9/9

When I See A Windmill In Al Gore's Front Yard…Then I'll Believe It
when I see a windmill. Standing there true-blue. stoic on it's stand
When I see a windmill, I think of West Texas' bold, strong-willed, honest

when I see a windmill I remember about Don Quixote
How could I not react **when I see a windmill**?
When I see a windmill I am reminded of God's great love

When I see a windmill, I see the symbol first
when I see a windmill or a whirligig toy, I get the giggle fits
I hear someones voice, a sound of a train, even **when I see a windmill**

all our lives we try

All our lives we try to find a way back to our innocence
All our lives we try Reach the sky to find the reason
all our lives we try to learn it as completely as possible
all our lives we try to make other people happy
All our lives we try and muffle the internal noise

(and dare I say, in **all our lives) & we try** to seize complete control
All our lives we try to balance the demands of our practical lives
All our lives we try to emulate God and behave like Him
having worked in and breathed media **all our lives. We try** to spot trends
All our lives, we try to find the melody in our own paths

All our lives we try to do right so we can raise and provide for our families
its saying how **all our lives we try** adn be the best we can
All our lives we try to build utopia
All our lives we try hiding
the sound that we look for **all our lives, we try** to compensate

My 2 sons and I have been ND fans **all our lives. we try**
All our lives we try to make marks on it, but it's hard
and **all our lives we try** to get the fish to swim
we've been friends for **all our lives. We try** to stay out of trouble
All our lives we try to tame reality by telling stories

All our lives we try to plan for the future to lessen the burden
Surely **all our lives we try** to be the best we can be
All our lives we try to hold on to things we love, people we cherish
All our lives, we try so hard to maximize some potential
All our lives, we try to recreate our childhoods

if only we would think

19/19

If only we would think before we act. but then
If only we would "think of taxes as spinach
if only we would think clearly

if only we would think of small rather than melting
If only we would think of how will this be taken
if only we would think, it would help us bear our burdens
and to achieve abundance **if only we would think** positively

If only we would think for ourselves and stop allowing the media to
if only we would think on our own for ourselves
If only we would think of the consequence of action in the context
If only we would think a little into the wonders
if only we would think of it

if only we would think big and give up
if only we would think differently
if only we would think we would be thankful
if only we would think with the bugbear of religion behind us

if only we would think of its effect of our kids
If only we would think of Christianity more as a grace, in which
more than enough food to go round the world **if only we would think**

hello am thinking

20/20

Hello am thinking about renovating my bathroom
Hello! Am thinking about doing some mini-tri's

Hello, Am thinking of becoming a contributor
hello" am thinking about'cha!

Hello! Am thinking of coming but how much is it
hello am thinking of calling A meeting

hello,am thinking of getting my bike a high flow air filter
Oh, **hello....am thinking** that I should really be doing the ironing

hello. am thinking about buying a e39 m5 and am asking
hello. Am thinking of you and hope

Hello! Am thinking about opening a women's oasis
hello am thinking about staying at a place called the chalets at boot

Hello! Am thinking of a DIFFERENT kind of Christmas turkey!
Hello, Am thinking of giving TS I try

Hello, am thinking of teaching my 2yr 4month son at home
Hello: Am thinking we are distant cousins

So wanted to say hello...am thinking of you guys lots
Hello Am thinking about buying a Pace 2600 digibox

Hello, Am thinking of staying at Hotel Club Nautico
Hello Am thinking of setting up a small website for our school

# of this particular future

on account **of this particular future**
the consequences **of this particular future** for arms control,
political and technological landscape **of this particular future**
stunning developments **of this particular future**. But Tyler

could determine unilaterally and hence know aspects **of this particular future** is
a viable operational reality **of this particular "future** for librarians"
of this particular future event at this particular moment

the thought **of this particular future** punishment can not afflict him
This means that the contract size **of this particular future** is
critical to primary care practice, the success **of this particular future**
now the lynchpin **of this particular future** history
an awful lot **of this particular future**'s potential

for Stranger did not match up to the rest **of this particular future**,
because of the strange capitalistic society **of this particular future**
motivated by the absence **of this particular future**, by the fact
all) of the other components **of this particular future** event
were involved in the process and result **of this particular future**

the success **of this particular future** alliance will
because **of this particular future** that 'the present is lived in total
gratuitous implication **of this particular future**, one worthy of
the case **of this particular future** event, I viewed it either as
some idea **of this particular future**: 'Worldwide Information Control

assured of the certainty **of this particular "future"**
gave us a little taste **of this particular future** that night. Big time.

is there some other explanation for his depiction **of this particular future**?

for Alien and Dick for Blade Runner] vision **of this particular future**
a belief in or a forecast **of this particular future**. The environment
of this particular Future Batman is undoutedly changed

This means that the contract size **of this particular future**
may be as significant a part **of this particular future**
to women that would accompany the arrival **of this particular "future**

as we all emerge

as we all emerge from winter
As we all emerge into a new year, ripe
As we all emerge from the same bunker
as we all emerge from a scarcely snowed-upon
snow and cold are finally gone and **as we all emerge**
has to evolve to survive, especially **as we all emerge**

As we all emerge from a hard winter, the call of spring
and even prosper **as we all emerge** from this event
the truth **as we all emerge**/evolve through the chasm

As we all emerge from this recession one of the main supports
is the glow of opportunity **as we all emerge** into the sun
soon...**as we all emerge** into the one true...we merge
as we all emerge into the back garden and swagger

As we all emerge from this time of economic
opening up across the board **as we all emerge**

As we all emerge from winter's drudge, it's time to plan
hopping again **as we all emerge** from the holidays
as we all emerge from this economy, we will
As we all emerge from the dark winter months feeling
wishes for the spring **as we all emerge** from our winter

As we all emerge from the same bunker, whether
As we all emerge from winter's drudge, it's time
As we all emerge from the Jackson-induced media
mode **as we all emerge** from the recession,
gradually getting back to normal **as we all emerge**

As we all emerge from the silly season,
As we all emerge from our Holy Week
in order to readjust for that, so **as we all emerge**
especially **as we all emerge**, shaken but not broken

chance to do it again i'd

70/70

If I had a **chance to do it again**, **I'd** do exactly the same
I'd love the **chance to do it again**. **I'd** love to keep my hand in
if I had the **chance to do it again**, **I'd** build it deeper
if you gave me a **chance to do it again**, **I'd** do it all the same way
If I had a **chance to do it again**, **I'd** probably have to say no [to that role]
it was wrong, if I had the **chance to do it again**, **I'd** probably still do drugs
You know, if I had a **chance to do it again I'd** be set up
If I had a **chance to do it again**, **I'd** have had an apartment alone
If I had a **chance to do it again**, **I'd** still buy the M1710!
If I get the **chance to do it again I'd** love to do it again
Given a **chance to do it again I'd** probably go into blood further
If I had the **chance to do it again**, **I'd** do it in a minute: I would recommend it
I got it done and if I had a **chance to do it again**, **I'd** definitely do it again
if I had the **chance to do it again**, **I'd** go whole hog
But if I had the **chance to do it again**, **I'd** definitely do a semester abroad
just want everyone to know if I had a **chance to do it again**, **I'd** still choose Seton
If I had a **chance to do it again**, **I'd** sing it again, better
If I had the **chance to do it again I'd** jump at it
a pleasure working with you, and I hope to have the **chance to do it again**. **I'd**
if I had the **chance to do it again I'd** change a lot of things. But all in all
If I had a **chance to do it again**, **I'd** make sure we protected parents
If Given the **chance to do it again**, **I'd** fight with you ,til the end
If I get the **chance to do it again I'd** love to do it again
If I had a **chance to do it again**, **I'd** try to see everything
If I had the **chance to do it again I'd** use a primer, and high gloss latex
You might not ever get the **chance to do it again**. **I'd**
have had my moments and if i had the **chance to do it again I'd** have more
ok, if I had a **chance to do it again**, **I'd** go a slightly different route

kind of fun at first, and if offered the **chance to do it again**, **I'd** refuse

If I had a **chance to do it again**, **I'd** just hold onto them all

if I had a **chance to do it again** **I'd** do it in a heartbeat

if i had a **chance to do it again** **I'd** practise interval/chord recognition

if given the **chance to do it again**, i,d buy plane tickets tomorrow § dance

if given the **chance to do it again**, **I'd** jump on him in a heartbeat

If I had a **chance to do it again**, **I'd** do it again," he said at the time

Given the **chance to do it again**, **I'd** probably do it differentl

If I had the **chance to do it again**, **I'd** search around

If I had the **chance to do it again**, **I'd** respond with more determination

If I had a **chance to do it again**, **I'd** include this: (3) Dismantle the LADOT

But given the **chance to do it again**, **I'd** go with a set of E code hellas or bosch

and given the **chance to do it again**, **I'd** do it the exactly the same

and if I had a **chance to do it again**, **I'd** do it again

given the **chance to do it again**, **I'd** call a locksmith

but if I had a **chance to do it again**, **I'd** say yes in a flash

if I had the **chance to do it again**, **I'd** probably re-mount them

he had the **chance to do it again**. **I'd** tracked him down to the Halkin

if I had any **chance to do it again**, **I'd** like to ride with a bigger engine

if I had the **chance to do it again** **I'd** choose the same setup

If I had the **chance to do it again**, **I'd** have a 50 on the inside

If I had a **chance to do it again** **I'd** say 'yes'

You know, if I had a **chance to do it again**, **I'd** make the same choices

Given the **chance to do it again**, **I'd** just donate everything to charity

and if given the **chance to do it again**, **I'd** jump on that in a hearbeat!

the money and the **chance to do it again**, **I'd** _still_ send them to that nursery

If I had a **chance to do it again**, **I'd** go for at least F14

if I had the **chance to do it again**, **I'd** go civu all the way. Degree before joining!

Personally, if we had the **chance to do it again**, **I'd** go to Atlantis

If I had the **chance to do it again** **I'd** insist on front and rear bars

Yet, given the **chance to do it again**, **I'd** say yes in a minute

f I had the **chance to do it again**, **I'd** go the same way

(Cont.)

If I had the **chance to do it again**, **I'd** go w/X50 without a second's hesitation

if they had the **chance to do it again**, **I'd** bet my house and car that they would

If I had a **chance to do it again**, **I'd** still put 5 into booster. attacking faster

given a **chance to do it again**, **I'd** go with the banana bread pudding!

had a **chance to do it again I'd** want to show my support

If I had a **chance to do it again**, **I'd** do a much better job

However, given a **chance to do it again**, **I'd** probably consider the following:

if I had a **chance to do it again**, **I'd** probably take the extra year

But if I had a **chance to do it again**, **I'd** keep music a priority